Meet Me Out There

Meet Me Out There

Poems by

Shutta Crum

© 2023 Shutta Crum. All rights reserved.
This material may not be reproduced in any form, published,
reprinted, recorded, performed, broadcast,
rewritten or redistributed without
the explicit permission of Shutta Crum.
All such actions are strictly prohibited by law.

Cover design by Shay Culligan
Cover image by Matthew Henry via Unsplash

ISBN: 978-1-63980-445-0

Kelsay Books
502 South 1040 East, A-119
American Fork, Utah 84003
Kelsaybooks.com

To the members of the poetry critique groups I have been in
over the years: you have all encouraged me, challenged me,
and befriended me. You have helped to shape my life
and brought so much joy into it, and for that
I am so grateful.
To friendship and poetry!

Acknowledgments

A special thanks goes out to Betsy Baier who continues to use her eagle eyes on these offerings, making sure they are fit for your eyes. And, of course, I owe so much that cannot be put into words to my very own poetry man, Gerry Clark.

Finally, I bow humbly to the many literary journals who do such a great job printing, distributing, and generally encouraging poems—even on shoestring budgets and with small staffs. I am grateful to the following journals for publishing the poems listed below. Thank you!

—SC

3rd Wednesday: "Leaving the Lake," "Small Boats"
AAR2: "August Ode to Innocence"
Blue Mountain Review: "Beneath Snow"
Boulevard: "Lesser Jewels"
Cadence, 2022 (FSPA): "Meet You Out There"
Calyx: "What They Wore"
Driftwood: "Still Life: A Portrait"
Fruition (North Fl. Poetry Hub): "Thirst"
A Gathering of Poets, Vol. #2: "Where I Work"
Making Waves: "Running Doesn't Matter"
Mom Egg Review: "Venus," "Demeter and the Corporate Good Ol' Boys"
North Florida Poetry Hub: "One Winter's Day"
Of Poets & Poetry: "Make Bread," under the title "Wasn't That a Dainty Dish"
The Orchards Poetry Journal: "Witness (With Friend)"
Peninsula Poets (Poetry Soc. of Michigan): "Unfinished Work"
West Trade Review: "The Scab," "Sternum"

Contents

Meet Me Out There   13
Just Go!   14

This Echo of a Daughter

First Mother   17
August Ode to Innocence   18
Venus   19
Running Doesn't Matter   20
God's Second Thought   21
Make Bread   23
My Mother Taught Me to Quilt   24

As Lovely as the Ache

Unfinished Work   27
Unlocking the Door   28
A Country of Temptations   29
Lesser Jewels   30
At the Vintage Shop   31
Grandpa Sings His Song   32

It Takes Time to Learn to Love

Am This   35
Sternum   36
Morning   37
Envelopes   38
Where I Work   39
One Winter's Day   40
The Half-Life of a Test Orbit   41
Georgia by the Window   43

The Space That Grief Takes Up

Still Life: A Portrait	47
Demeter and the Corporate Good Ol' Boys	48
What They Wore	49
Newton's Laws :: Angles > Angels	50
The Scab	52
Witness (with Friend)	53

Pending the Passage

Leaving the Lake	57
Death Comes for Dinner	58
Small Boats	59
Subsidence	60
Things Done Wrong	61
The Last Synaptic Hurrah	62
Reflected in the Cloud Gate	63
Lift Me Unto the Grasslands	64
I'm Not All Here Today	65

Meet Me Out There

There's a space between breaths where we might touch.
And before we speak, there's a small meadow of silence.
Let's meet out there.
We can stand beside rivers that have always known
where they are going.

It won't matter if we slip into the water.
Each stumble is an acknowledgement of earth, and of sky—
that vast wonder that starts down by our feet and rises and rises.
It's always there to welcome our return.

Besides, it's wise
to leave wet footprints trailing through the fields.
They're a way to find each other, should we need finding.
What do you say? Let's meet again, and again.

There's a good spot at the willowy edges of words
where the meadow grass is tall
and the wildflowers are shameless and drunk on sunshine.

Just Go!

doesn't matter where
it's the music of the pavement
the faces of people you pass
trees that bend to bless you

the road always beckons
with a force that thrusts
through muscle, plunges
into lungs, says: this one's alive

keep windows down
hail the woosh of wind
its cool challenge on your neck
the landscapes whizzing by

the growl of tires spitting gravel
the hurtle into potholes
the weightless rise out again
the righting after

cheer all the evenings
that have crept into your pores
and yield to any dawn
sitting sassy on the horizon

the tank is full enough
it's the mystery of the road
no matter what the odometer reads
or where the compass points

This Echo of a Daughter

First Mother

She is haloed in the dawn.
Dark figure limned in gold,
one bare foot after another
out of the African highlands.
The gathering light reveals
she is with child.

First Mother
who crossed deserts,
pulled herself up mountains—
then rested her feet on two continents.
In the east a vast grassland billowed.
In the west river valleys beckoned.

Mother of daughters—
each a passageway into the future.
Each lifting children in torchlight
and pressing small palms
against cave walls—
red-ocher signaling
we came this way.

In the day's first light
I stretch my hands out,
turning them over and over.
I see a landscape
of scars and callouses—
a history of crisscrossed continents.
And I cry out with simple words,
hoping she will hear
this echo of a daughter.

I want her to know I made it.

August Ode to Innocence

Perhaps it was the timbre of the afternoon and the incessant thrumming of cicadas. Or the slant of light through maple leaves—resting, a moment, on your eyes. Perhaps it was the way the smell of mown grass confused my senses. Or maybe it was the feel of your summons against my neck—an open invitation whispered as we lay on a blanket. It may have been all these things—or none of them. Still, that summer I came willingly, sliding my bare feet through the blur and blush of August—only catching the glisten in my mother's eye a moment, before I slipped away.

Venus

There she is—pale Lucifer,
the morning star.
(Not the mis-translated other
who fell from Heaven.
This one's firmly in place.)

I raise a finger and touch
the cold glass through which I see
our companion planet.
And I wonder about the light
of a younger world—

before I birthed myself
from the salt and the silt,
might I have seen the daystar
flickering on the waves above me?

Might I have taken
that first painful gulp of air
as I caught her in the dawning?
Might I have called out
(as I sometimes do now)
for reassurance before day
donned its bright mask?

Might I have lain like a thing dead,
not knowing the miracles to come,
and awaited her in the dimming—
my Hesperus (Venus of the evening).

And there she is, a pledge I hold on to
in the rolling tilt of the night sky,
just past the tip of my finger—
lodged in the heart of this thing I have become.

Running Doesn't Matter

You'll get here—
where pools are memory deep.
Where you can stir the waters with a toe,
or lie on your stomach and drink.

I know you might not hear this
the way I want you to hear it.
Or feel it, the way I want you to—
as a whisper through sun-bleached antler,
as the breath of a promise under moon-rush.
Or as a mothering call from painted cliffs.

I might not be saying it correctly.
It's just that I know you'll get here—
where regrets soften,
where the practiced eye is keener,
where the fern moss sweetens each step,
and you can touch what you couldn't
when the world whistled urgently at your back.

Run, only if you must.
I'll be waiting here by a white birch.
I'll hold you as you catch your breath.
I'll lead you to the water,
and wash your weary feet
in the cooling prayers of an ancient grace.

God's Second Thought

What the hell do I do with this rib?

I imagine God said something like that
as Adam lay bleeding at his feet.
Perhaps the Almighty, momentarily startled,
waved the rib about hoping for a quick idea.
Perhaps He flung it as the first boomerang
and found it was wayward—falling, defiantly,
and knocking an apple from a tree.

Perhaps, having retrieved the rib,
He stood glorious in a shaft of light
and saw how elegant, how smooth it was.
How strong. And yet, how fragile.

Perhaps Adam groaned while clutching his side
and disturbed God's godly thoughts.
Then the Holy One had a second idea about mankind—
why not a helpmate? Someone to nurse that first one,
to stop his bleeding.

And while He was at it,
why not someone to rub His own haggard back?
Someone to tell Him what to do when He lost his thoughts—
or got lost in them, what with all those heavy dinosaurs
and frantic amoebas mucking about.

Certainly, the Alpha and the Omega
could use someone to tell Adam to get over it.
So, God slid heavenly fingers along that shapely bone
and declared, *Of course! I'll create Eve.*

Later, His work done, the Divine One likely trotted home
with a good dog for company
thinking, surely, there'd be a hot meal and maybe—even—
a warm piece of pie waiting. Made by that latest lovely human.

Finally, I imagine God coming into His house
and stopping on the rug to wipe the nasty things
He'd created off his shoes.
Perhaps Adam limps in after and the two of them
stare at the empty plates, the can of beans, the can-opener
on the countertop, and at the apple on the table—
half-eaten.

Make Bread

Sprinkle a few tears on some yeast and let it proof.
Then get out the stainless-steel bowl
you took from your mother's house after she died.
It's dented and cold to the touch.
Dump in 4 cups of unbleached memory—
the sweetness of summer apples,
autumn rain, and the warmth of an evening fire.

Whisk together until you see your mother eating an apple,
or standing lovely by a bonfire—in the rain.
Cut in a bit of her laughter until pea-sized.
In a smaller bowl temper your thoughts with clarified moments.

Did she hold you when your dog Bugsy died?
Did you once see her kissing the neighbor?
Make a well in your memories, pour in your thoughts.
Leaven honestly with the yeast you proofed.
Mix until it comes together—large, and heavy,
and you can barely lift it.

Now, turn it out onto a surface dusted with words
you wish you'd spoken. Knead, recalling
the baseball games she never came to,
the school play she couldn't be bothered with.
Let it rise until doubled. Then punch it down. Let it rest.

Go outside, breathe in the air scented with winter.
Wander a while remembering the fragrance of apples.
Return to the dough and tuck the troubled edges under.
Shape it in a way that pleases you—the way you tucked blankets
around her that autumn when it rained, and she slipped away.
Let it all rise again. Then bake it in the oven of your heart.

Pair this with a good Zinfandel.
One with a complex bouquet, and undernotes of regret.

My Mother Taught Me to Quilt

—for Evelyn Crum (1933–2008), master quilter

My mother taught me to quilt—
how to measure width and length,
how to find shades of a rainy day,
or the hue of a child's trust.
I watched as she patched each day's pieces
into a kaleidoscopic whole.
And she always saved the scraps.

She taught me to ease dissonance
into harmonies of pattern, and to blind stitch.
She tugged, and I saw, that the straight grain was strong.
But she said I must learn to work with bias,
for there are days when fabric needs to stretch.

I studied how she smoothed the layers—
how she rocked her needle, hand-stitching
it all to a strong back. And finally,
how she held me bundled in her patchwork.

Now, on rainy days
I walk out onto the wet grass and collect
my colors—the impatient greens, the heart-deep browns,
the glistening grays, and the fresh-washed blue of a forget-me-not.
I measure. I cut. I rock my needle.
I bind my raw edges.

As Lovely as the Ache

Unfinished Work

I write to capture your voice,
still tut-tutting over this, or that, unfinished work.
To hear the soft lilt of it clearly
as it wafts through summer, lingers in autumn,
splashes syllable by syllable, into the pond.

I write to hold on—
as your echo leaps over farmlands,
wanders through woodlots, rises on the breath
of fawns and their mothers in swirled beds of switchgrass.

I write because afternoons are fading.
And there are too few times
when I can capture your cadences
and wear them like a second skin.

I write to learn the timbre of what I'm becoming,
to acquiesce to your wisdom. Though gone,
you're still singing as you pin my hems up, make my lunches.
So, I straighten my shoulders, steady my feet—
only sometimes wobble, longing to hear a satisfied word.

I write, listening to you hum—
knowing one day this work will be finished.

Unlocking the Door

—for Melvin Crum (1925–2008)

My father opened doors. Telling me,
You can be anything you want.
This from a man who could not read.
This from a man whose lungs were blackened,
whose hands were thick and veined
like the seams of coal he worked.
This from a man who learned to run
faster on his knees than he did on his feet.
This from a man who made sure I could read
and walk unhindered in the world.

Even when he could no longer unlock my name,
he knew his love for me was his diamond in the coal.
This man, who lifted me over so many thresholds—
>	patiently waited at the memory-care home
>	for me to step through the opened door.

A Country of Temptations

swept together in windrows
along crowded hallways
the boys I remember
had thumbs hooked in back pockets
feet planted, or ankles casually crossed
they leaned against lockers
or balanced books on hips
thigh muscles straining against denim
shoulders broadening into manhood

how I loved the shocks of hair yanked over brows
like the thrill of an impending storm
or flipped across faces like summer wheat blown astray
how I loved their wrists, tanned and strong
and smiles that opened slow, sly, knowingly
smiles that haunted my travels down corridors

how I roamed—my breath held
through a country of temptations
a land contoured with mystery
alive with all those beautiful bodies of boys
and how I dared to dream of them
yearning for one who might reach out
might cup my shoulders, pull me close
unfurl the need in me
and become the compass I so wanted in that wilderness

Lesser Jewels

Cloudy topaz, crazed quartz, chipped garnet.
We were the lesser stars of the firmament.
We were the door-slamming, *Up-yours!*
The mouthy girl enigmas.
All long-legs, bared midriffs. Skirts hiked up.

Not cheerleaders, not scholars.
Not Future Homemakers of America.
We were the rough cuts—
the backseat business
in the fields behind the school.
The semi-precious
dancing in the headlights,
our bodies tripwire and baited spark.

Wild-haired, breasty.
The ones tonguing boys. The teasers.
Hoots and hollers the polish
of fame we could almost touch—
a possibility of luster.

We were the pretenders
shoving hurt into overstuffed lockers,
faux leather purses—faux smiles.
Revelers in a second-hand radiance.
Everything we had, already used
by the richer, purer, more refined.

But we could strut hand-me-downs,
smile a *Thank you!* and a *Fuck-off!*
at the same time,
while shoplifting what we wanted.
We were lesser jewels. But in the right light—
my, God! What brilliance.

At the Vintage Shop

I slip my feet into high heels
—sling-backs, peek-a-boo toe.
And I'm happy, wondering who bought these.
New in the 1950s? 60s?
And did she buy a sundress, too?
I stretch the baggy fabric of my sweatpants,
shaping an imaginary dress, and I twirl—
certain that these shoes were worn
with a frock. One as lovely and bold as sunflowers.

The right shoe slants a little left.
The left slants a bit right.
She was someone who leaned into herself.
Perhaps her legs were weak
from a childhood illness, or a life of hard work.
Did she wear these special shoes as often as possible?
Perhaps to see the man she loved.
Perhaps to cross her legs and tease,
with a bit of scarlet polish peeking out.

I've no place to wear them—
these cherished riches of a young woman.
They're not meant for me.
I buy them anyway.

Grandpa Sings His Song

When Grandpa Wells sings
his face is at peace above a faded shirt,
frayed pants, stretched suspenders.
And we who listen are suspended somewhere high
in the green arms of the mountains,
in a far-off time and place when the world
welcomed traveling minstrels—songwriters
from whom you could buy a song written just for you.

In the hush around us, aunts quietly set pots of green beans
with ham hocks, platters of biscuits, and pies on the table.
They wipe hands on dishrags, adjust housedresses. Wait. Listen.
Uncles spit tobacco juice into paper cups,
and stop their low conversations to look up.
Children squirm closer—five generations—
though we can't understand a word of the song.
Toothless, Grandpa sings.

He is as ancient as the pale outcroppings
that surround us. Wind-scoured and etched
by years of hard work, by a constancy of the heart—
as much a part of these weathered hills
as mountain laurel, moss, and the ghostly tatters of fog.

Now, everything about him is dimming.
But I still see his hands, resting on the top of his cane.
They are lichened by liver spots, but strong.
And his song, accompanied by the murmurs of the creek,
the nodding of heads, and the curious whispers of children,
is just as lovely as the ache left in its wake.

It Takes Time to Learn to Love

Am This

            :: a fieldling
in the way the world is
why not a horse?
the bulging eye watchful
and you, grazing beside me

or am this :: the way summer exhales
its breath :: lingering in dry grasses
a summons
beguiling :: your muscled flanks
lifting and settling
in the heat of a tawny distance

or this :: the bitten lip :: the red hands
in gray dishwater :: the worried lodger
renting this heart

or this :: the call from the farmhouse
above fields of timothy and clover
scurried along on the breeze :: a tugging
until you turn toward home

and this :: a bowl of strawberries
an apron fluttering :: a confession
a penance

Sternum

breastbone :: stout sentry

heart   burdened
my ribs have borne years
even that borrowed bone
bruised   but vigilant
rises with breath
              the breastbone
stalwart, pulls heartward
keeps this body aright

born unfused
the sternum   soft pieces
it takes time to learn to love
to become
hardened :: defender :: warder
      of inhabitants of the heart
and of those who rent space
for a while

        sometimes
            I walk out heavy
under the stars and wonder
how it might feel to bash this bone
against infinite light
      to rise   empty

challenged
      I place my hand :: pale scout
between my breasts   feel the armor

Morning

I rub liniment
into your shoulders,
hips, knees, and ankles—
lingering over each part of you.

Your eyes
are half open in the pink light
beckoning
through the bedroom window.

Later, I bring you an egg
and toast.
And in an old spoon
I offer raspberry jam—
thick, seedy,
and scandalously red.

Envelopes

The first arrives at dusk on the 15th. It slides under my door
and contains a single sheet. A single line. *I've gone missing.*

I stare out the kitchen window. Who's gone? Why tell me?
From the yard, a bird I don't recognize
chastises me. So, I think of you.
You were always going to end up missing.

I study the envelope. No return address.
Maybe it's not from you. You need an audience.
Even in the cul-de-sac where we pedaled Big Wheels—
superheroes in tiny bodies. You, deliberately crashing.

The second envelope arrives two evenings later
with a single sheet, a single line.
Three words, again. *I'm walking blind.*

Walking? Where? Through the sullen cast-offs of night?
To stagger into the arms of the wrong shadow?
In the dark I lie awake thinking of this bookmark
you've left in another chapter of my life,
knowing the stories you love end up mangled, bloody.

For days, I scratch at obstinate scars. They itch,
wanting—and not wanting—another envelope.
Muscles tensing at a distant child's cry,
at the screech of brakes, at the strength of the wind
threatening to loosen the battens
of that hold I pushed you into years ago.

Through the jangle of rivaling skies, I slip away
before another message arrives.
Leaves skitter. In the distance, the clamor of sirens.

Where I Work

Over there is a book I haven't read.
But there's another with worn pages
feathered cottony. *Medieval Lives*—
women working, as do I.

On a shelf is an origami box—empty.
No bit of down awaiting a broody.
No disembodied *tuk-tuk-tuk* to fret about.
No micro-turbulence to avoid.

Above that, school photos perch
in the frames of other pictures.
A bevy of smiles nested
into busy lives.

From a vase water tracks
around the clock's heartbeat
and down to the teardrop eye
roosted in a peacock's plume—
dusty cerulean and indigo.

And half-hidden,
a bent wing . . .

. . . that hard winter
we crested the hill and flew
all the way across the frozen pond.

One Winter's Day

How quietly we stood
With snowflakes in our hair
And watched the fox
Step through the wood

It came so close we could
Feel its breath like prayer
Two lovers and a fox
How quietly we stood

The Half-Life of a Test Orbit

—for Will Robinson, Flash Gordon, and David Bowie

Imagine a boy lost in a constellation of ghosts.
His mother gone in a millisecond of time and space,
her second-best shoes neatly on the rug.
Do ghosts come back for shoes?
Imagine his father bringing home boxes of cereal.
Never, any milk.
The boy wonders if ghosts
and the heavy questions they carry
float weightless among the stars.

Imagine the grass, cold and wet
against bare feet.
And the boy with a dry wind
whimpering through his ribs.
He hears a voice
from a distant quarter of the night.
"Danger! Danger, Will Robinson!"
Questions sprout from him
into a tangle of thorns, desperately heavy.
He lifts his eyes from the nettles
and traces Orion's belt with a finger.

Imagine Flash Gordon
to the left of the Horsehead Nebula
making a 90-degree right turn
and a soft landing in this impossible thicket.
He presses past thorns, through tendrils,
sinking into skin, and skull,
until his capsule-shaped spaceship
rides synaptic pulses.
Flash Gordon waves from a porthole
and the boy's heart, once ebbing, rallies.

Imagine the night, star-tufted.
Elon Musk's Tesla is orbiting the Earth
and one small boy.
The driver's a tattered angel, a starman
who once fell to Earth,
and loved a woman who left him.
Starman has no answers for the boy,
only a trunk full of Cheerio boxes
in a Roadster riding solar winds.

Georgia by the Window

—for Georgia O'Keeffe

he took photos of you—a delicate sylph unfolding, rising
your ribs lifting small breasts into muted light
your pubic hair claiming the shadows, a wanton nest of dark
but you were never his insubstantial creature of the air

it took the desert to uncover the taut brown crux of yourself
it took relentless sun to leather you until you were thorn, and true
it took the sweep of black skirts over bleached bone
and sturdy boots, laced tight, to paint the Sangre de Cristo
    Mountains

his camera did get your hands right—those spidery fingers
long, arched—strong enough to defy light, to strip down
to the naked weight of what is sacred

The Space That Grief Takes Up

Still Life: A Portrait

She leans her cheek against the screen of the door,
stares at the pitted concrete steps and the curlicued iron rail.

She feels herself inside her skin, loose,
the meat of her too shriveled for this life.

There is no comfort here—only rattle and gristle,
and an alarming smallness.

She has walked through this house without touching it.
Now, at the door, she sacrifices skin to wire mesh.

Down the block, a child is playing heedless
of the intimacies of sunlight, or the impertinence of the wind.

She's been schooled in the hush through which she carries herself,
in the lost mission of fingerprints, in the soft-footed slouch of time.

The door, unaccustomed to this touch, is lost in its own thoughts.

Demeter and the Corporate Good Ol' Boys

the oil in the grain went rancid
the bread rose, gall-like and bitter
she served it anyway
the dust in their mouths
the taste of Demeter's revenge

raped by Zeus, the CEO of the whole shebang
her daughter taken to the underworld
given gladly by her father to his brother Hades

but soon, the gods got to thinking their grain-mother
was overworking this whole grief thing
why let the crops die, the fruit wither

come home, the corporation's good ol' boys said
straightening their crowns and golden wreaths
clicking their pens and looking efficient
there's work to be done, they said
we'll send you a train ticket

why dress in black, why wander
without an oven to call your own
Persephone was a ripe young thing
she's fine—even ate some pomegranate seeds

look, here's your daughter now—hold her
while you can, let the green world flourish
and the bread be sweet again
you won't have to say good-bye for . . .
shall we say six months?

that-a-girl

What They Wore

—Srebrenica, 1995–1996

the precious book is opened flat
balanced on three pairs of knees
the sisters—close, tense—brush fingertips across each page

murmurs rise, heads shake nervously
a lip is bitten as they inspect images
first, a picture of a shirt, mud-stained, torn

splayed and pinned against a white background
then, a pair of children's sneakers, no laces
one flipped on its side, dirty pink

the women turn pages slowly, so slowly
unsure if that is the vest Katya knitted for uncle
before he went for milk, never came back

each numbered photograph a too-bright gasp of light
the book, a first step with each mass grave
do you recognize this apron? this belt? these boots?

do you recognize this yellow sweater with worn cuffs?
difficult to look—to see the small and personal uncovered
forlorn, dirtied, tacked against all that clean white

the women turn another page. . . *Majčin šal*
Mother's scarf? two of the women lean closer
the third squeezes her eyes tight, groans

the scarf in the photograph is unfurled, blue
together, the sisters fall forward
hugging the book between knees and breasts

beside them wait others, silently rocking from foot to foot
they do not look at the women—at the space their grief takes up
but each will step forward soon to turn the pages

Newton's Laws :: Angles > Angels

*—for the young victims of Uvalde, Oxford, Nickel Mines,
Parkland, Newtown, Columbine...*

(w)racked :: head in hands
no angels on the morning shift today
I know the laws of nature predict trajectories

1.

Newton's first law
*an object moves in a straight line
unless acted upon by a force*

the angle of fire stopped by a child
nothing for angels to rejoice in
I scarcely believe in them, anyway
only in the absolute of small coffins

2.

Newton's second law
*the acceleration of an object is directly related
to the net force and inversely related to the mass*

net force :: anger > angels
each bullet weighing so little
the smaller it is, the faster it goes
in Nickel Mines the girls lined up :: pop! :: pop!

> Hey, NRA, quite contrary,
> How does your garden grow?
> With silver bells, and cockle shells
> And pretty little ones in a row.

angels have no weight in this equation

3.

Newton's third law
for every action there is an equal and opposite reaction

no :: the old man of science is wrong
unless someone's weighing the implosion of hearts
      :: no ::

politicians angle dirty white hats :: stick to their guns
bestow moments of silence :: prayer
      callously debate

how many angels can dance on the head of a firing-pin

The Scab

when i'm not
singing along
with birds
or with the plink
of rain
in a metal bucket
i absently pick
at the scab
trying to ease
the edge up to see
if the skin beneath
has begun to heal

no—it's a hurt
that's chosen
to haunt
this body

decades i've flown
more or less
at the altitude
designated for
middle-class women
having had
no mindless horror
inflicted
no turbulence
of broken bones
and when i wobble
i level out
from a good tailwind

yet, unguarded
i pick at it
always surprised

to find
I wasn't
gouged
in a dream
and that the ghost
of a pain
can linger
so long
fifty years
have not
weathered it
to dust

when I catch
myself
scratching and prying
the ground rushes up

and the dark
rises sickly
into its old home
in my throat

Witness (with Friend)

I'll put my coat on and join you.

>See the farm field? How the snow
>shapes and shadows it,
>hugging the furrowed clay—
>no matter how many seasons it lies fallow.

The surfaces of things glisten.

>But beneath that flimsy veil
>the wild mustard and burdock have died back,
>the scratchings of paw and hoof are hidden.
>The snow belies its gentle demeanor—
>the old, hard ruts are still there.

We both know that.

>Wind, rain, hail may scour and scuff the earth,
>but there's little that pummeling can do
>to smooth the way for someone who's fallen
>on the stubble of an old pain. For someone
>who walks that field every day.

We won't throw a hopeful dawn upon it.

>Clods and briers rise up
>through thin disguises.
>The puckered field always catches an ankle,
>grabs at a heart.

So, give me your hand.

Pending the Passage

Leaving the Lake

In an uprush of wings, wild geese are abandoning the lake.
They rise with their cries of *are you coming?*
Lifting from the watery reflections of maple and alder,
each finds its place in the slanting light.

I, too, feel Winter's approach,
hear her stealing through the evening hours,
see her white breath curl and swell across the water,
know her handiwork in the filigree lacing the shallows.

So, I'm chinking the splintered gaps in the old house,
bringing in the firewood, restocking the larder.
I promise to stay as long as I can.
I thought you'd want to know.

When the snow deepens, I'll put on your sweater.
The sleeves, too long, will shelter my hands.
I'll walk the path to the water.
The last of the geese will have gathered in the mist.

They'll stretch their necks, lift heavy bottoms,
slap the lake into a frenzy of silver,
and cry out as they veer off over the pines,
Are you coming? Are you coming?

Death Comes for Dinner

You weren't invited. But here you are.
With your green coat, stained and loose over skinny shoulders.
The lining's a dirt-brown plaid. You haven't shaved.
At the table I pass you a platter of tender days
spent picking apples, swimming in the river, studying clouds.
You make a face, wave the dish away. It isn't what you came for.

The silence grows awkward. I can hear the clock
in the foyer. It's racing, trying to catch up with my heart.
So, I offer an old story of driving through a blizzard.
A whiteout so thick there's only a small tunnel telescoping
to gray road eked out by the car's snow-covered headlights.

Your eyebrows rise into the brown thatch of your hair.
You grin slyly at me. I see that boyish dimple
in the shadows of your bristled cheek.
This is the sustenance you like, full of danger.
Fear another passenger in the backseat.
But when I finish by telling you of holding my grandchild,
born on that wintry January night, you yawn.
It's not the way you would have served up the story.

You rummage through pockets, retrieve a soiled handkerchief,
cough into it. I try not to notice blood, your weed-choked throat.
I stare at my knife, my fork, at the plate I've piled so much onto.
I take one more bite of a perfectly baked afternoon and say,
"If I'd known you were coming, I'd offer something special."

"You have," you tell me, delightedly waving your hand
over the length of the heavily laden table.
You lean close. I can smell your breath now—unexpectedly sweet.
"It's my delicate stomach," you explain. "I never partake.
I'll just keep you company, a while."

I consider the delicacies on my table, and smile.
"There's still dessert to be served," I say.

Small Boats

—for Mike

We are salt. We are water.
We carry brine through tributaries,
and feel the tides surge to the brain,
the fingertips, the toes.

I've read that the moon is inching away,
and that the Earth's spin is slowing—as are the tides.
Yet, clams in the Ohio River continue to feel them,
as do plants whose inner oceans, like ours,
respond to the moon's gravity.

And here, sitting by your side,
I worry that the rivers within you
are rushing too quickly to the sea.
Worry that someday, standing on shore,
I'll lose sight of you in the small boat of your body.

I lay a hand on your wrist—feel your skin
afloat above muscle and bone,
and know that what sustains us is water.
These waters upon which we've gambled everything
in such frail canoes.

Subsidence

—for Jayne

powerful forces inch through years of grand days
sun-buttered
snow-hushed
or heart-full
at the edges of oceans

there is no stopping tectonics—plates shift
fault lines crack
even as you stand watch
even as you monitor
     tremors

what was once outward
subsides down and in
it's a stealthy slide
     until

one day
     there's a seismic event
and the other side of the bed empties

Things Done Wrong

—for Mom (1933–2008)

Forgive me—
When you left, I forgot
to harvest the poems
that had taken root
in the floodplain of your hands.

I forgot to bathe
clear-eyed in the river-light
that buoyed your bed.

I forgot to fend off
that pale moon-faced tillerman—
nightshade tucked neatly
in his buttonhole—boat ready.

It is only now,
when I wake and wade into the river,
that I call out to that patient gentleman
Wait! Wait!
As though we were old friends.
As though he'd return
what was once mine.

The Last Synaptic Hurrah

There's a light, they say, at the end.
And a calm flowing feeling.
Scientists have studied this last synaptic hurrah—
illuminating the tunnelways of the brain,
flooding the body with serotonin.

Our impulses storm in the dark,
across the mind's vast universe.
It takes time for the lightning to wear itself out,
for the thunder to fade. But we know we're dying.

Some who return report floating,
watching the living below, hearing conversations.
I like to think I might drift out a window,
become the flicker of light dancing on your upturned hand.

Reflected in the Cloud Gate

—"Cloud Gate" by Anish Kapoor (the Chicago Bean)
in Millennium Park, Chicago, IL

this body distorts, stretches
with the curved green of the park
I've no idea if I'll rise—float
over parking lots, laundromats
above a father changing a tire
or sisters leaping through the spray of a sprinkler

perhaps I'll lift above my grandchildren
whose hands I grip at my side
perhaps I'll drift past open windows
smell cardamom and curry
or be buoyed out to the bay to be blown southward
down the fat cheeks of the continent

the children wiggle, make faces
not sensing a foreshadowed afterlife
a glimpse of a future, hushed, yet able to soar
above the Cloud Gate to rise on up-currents
or to settle in the harbor of cupped hands

but I acknowledge it—
hoping, as my grandchildren laugh
that I'll forever be able to run a thumb
along their determined little chins

Lift Me Unto the Grasslands

When I shake off this mammalian shape
I want to strip to naked seed.
I want to lift onto a passing breeze, hijack a ride
into the future on a dusty flank.

Like kindred ovules carried by mammoths,
early horses, aurochs—
the great grazers of the steppes,
I want to be quickened and cast out.
I want to feel my green spine momentous.

I'm Not All Here Today

Of course not—I float
into the milky mouths of children.
Issue from the wheezes of elders.
Soak into the stomata of trees.
Melt snow from the noses of elk.

As I stare into the dusk, writing,
I take in air from Denali and let it fill me.
Then, sighing, part of me hurries forth
to swirl about the summit of Everest,
to sculpt the singing dunes in the Gobi,
to bubble up from bayous.

What I inhale is the air of an early Earth,
drawn in and pushed out through eons.
What I exhale takes me with it.
There's no such thing as just being here—now.

I am everywhere, flirting—
with hydrogen, carbon, nitrogen.
I always have—from the first tiny bubble of lung
hanging from that first fragile bone.

That's why I'm not all here today.
That. And I'm taking a nap—just breathing—
in a hammock stretched between God's hands.

About the Author

Shutta Crum is an award-winning poet, Pushcart Prize nominee, and children's book writer, as well as an oft-requested speaker and presenter at writing conferences, libraries, and schools. Shutta's poems have appeared in many journals since the 1970s. Numerous poems have been published by the *AAR2* over the years. (The online Ann Arbor Review.) Other poems were published or are forthcoming in *Typehouse, Of Poets & Poetry, Orchards Poetry Journal, 3rd Wednesday, Acumen, Mom Egg Review, West Trade Review, Calyx,* and *Boulevard*. Her chapbook *When You Get Here* (2020) won a gold Royal Palm Literary Award. *The Way to the River* came out in 2022 from Kelsay Books. She is, also, the author of three novels for young readers and many children's picture books including *Thunder-Boomer!* (Clarion/HMH), a *Smithsonian Magazine* and an *American Library Association* notable book of the year. In 2005 she was a guest author at the White House Easter Egg Roll, and in 2010 she was invited to tour Japan presenting to the students of the Department of Defense schools.

Contact Shutta at:
Website ~ shutta.com
Facebook ~ facebook.com/Shuttacrum
Twitter ~ @Shutta
Instagram ~ instagram.com/Shuttacrum

Praise for *The Way to the River*
by Shutta Crum
(Chapbook, Kelsay Books, 2022)

Shutta Crum finds her way to the river, to baptism and redemption. She pulls up the stuff we've discarded—but also a few rainbows—before she floats in her playful heaven. She describes her journey in a language as clear as the water she hopes will carry her and her readers through the river's twists and turns.

  ~ Keith Taylor, A.L. Becker Collegiate Lecturer in English (retired) and Director, Bear River Writers' Conference (retired)

Praise for *When You Get Here*
by Shutta Crum
(Chapbook, Kelsay Books, 2020)

Here's everything you want in poetry. Understandable language—check. Interesting, inventive use of words—check. Topics that reference matters of common interest—check. Insights way beyond the usual—check. Don't skim this collection. You'd miss way too much that makes our lives meaningful. Enter and walk "unafraid in this new topography."

  ~ Sharon Scholl, Professor emerita of humanities and author of *Music and Culture, Death and the Humanities,* and five chapbooks of poetry

www.ingramcontent.com/pod-product-compliance
Lightning Source LLC
Chambersburg PA
CBHW030914170426
43193CB00009BA/846